MW01143314

V2T 5E1

Great Careers for People Interested in the

Performing Arts

by
Gillian Bartlett

An Imprint of Gale Research Inc.

Copyright © 1994
Trifolium Books Inc. and Weigl Educational Publishers Limited

First published in Canada by Trifolium Books Inc. and
Weigl Educational Publishers Limited

U.S. edition published exclusively by

An Imprint of
Gale Research Inc.
835 Penobscot Bldg.
Detroit, MI 48226

Library of Congress Catalog Card Number 94-60778
ISBN 0-8103-9964-4

The activities in this book have been
tested and are safe when carried out
as suggested. The publishers can
accept no responsibility for any
damage caused or sustained by use or
misuse of ideas or materials
mentioned in the activities.

Acknowledgments
The author and the publishers wish to
thank those people whose careers are
featured in this book for allowing us
to interview and photograph them at
work. Their love for their chosen
careers has made our task an
enjoyable one.

Design concept: Julian Cleva
Design and layout: Warren Clark
Editors: Sarah Swartz, Jane McNulty
Project coordinator, proofreader: Diane Klim
Production coordinator: Amanda Woodrow
Content review: Trudy Rising, Mary Kay Winter

Printed and bound in Canada
10 9 8 7 6 5 4 3 2 1

This book's text stock contains
more than 50% recycled paper.

Contents

Featured profiles

Actor

PERSONAL PROFILE

Career: Actor. "You take the audience out of their ordinary lives and trigger their imaginations."

Interests: Many. "I cycle. I enjoy drawing and painting. I love going to movies. I read a lot, mostly about other people's lives. And I write a bit. I even had an article published. I also like to play the piano when I get the chance."

Latest accomplishment: "I just got a leading role in a play. I'm thrilled because there was a lot of competition, and the part wasn't specifically written for a black actor."

Why I do what I do: "I enjoy seeing the world through somebody else's eyes."

I am: Interested in people. "Television programs like the news and talk shows let me see real-life reactions that I can sometimes use later in my acting."

What I wanted to be when I was in school: "As a child, I was always putting on plays with neighborhood kids. But I didn't decide on acting as a career until after high school."

What an actor does

"An actor is basically working every day," says Catherine. "Even when actors are not rehearsing specific roles, they'll be doing something to help their careers. Sometimes this means keeping in phone contact with people in the business. Sometimes it means taking a voice class. And it definitely means you check the call boards."

Before actors become successful enough to have agents, the call boards are their lifelines. These bulletin boards are located at theatrical union and association offices. Theater companies post notices for upcoming roles. Notices include a brief description of the roles needed for a play. They also include information such as where and when auditions will be held.

But film and television roles are rarely posted in this way. Instead, these roles are available only through talent agencies. When agents receive detailed notices of new roles, they look through the list of actors they represent and send the most suitable ones to the "call."

Auditioning

At theater auditions, actors are expected to deliver monologues — one- to two-minute excerpts from plays. "You normally have two or three different monologues ready that give some idea of your range," says Catherine.

What happens at an audition is unpredictable. "The last role I auditioned for was a character who changes in age from 15 to 27," reports Catherine. She knew that the director had already seen her in an older role on stage, so Catherine decided to prepare a speech that emphasized her youth. "But when I walked on stage and told the director what I was going to do, he asked me if I could do something from Shakespeare instead. I had to pull something out of my head really fast." Catherine decided to give one of Portia's speeches from *Julius Caesar* — and she got the role.

Preparing a role

Once an actor gets a part, the real work begins. It's important to read over the script several times. But an actor also needs to do research. "Researching a role can be really interesting," remarks Catherine enthusiastically. "Every character is a new learning experience. You have to find out what people in that line of work do. You've got to research the time period and determine how people behaved socially." Sometimes an actor must learn the basics of a new skill, such as playing a musical instrument, or dancing the tango, or even flying a kite.

Compared to the research and preparation, the amount of time an actor actually spends in performance can be very short. But the long hours of work that are involved before the performance are well worth the satisfaction that comes from entertaining an audience.

Catherine rides her bike as often as possible. "It's important to keep fit, because acting requires energy and flexibility."

"I find it's easiest to learn my lines once the director has worked out the blocking, and I can fit the words to actions," reports Catherine. Blocking involves decisions about where the actors will move and what they will do on stage.

All in a day's and night's work

In the first days of rehearsing a play, the director and the actors will do "table work." They read the play together and discuss the characters as though the characters were real people. How does their environment affect the characters? Why do the characters say what they say? What makes them act the way they do towards each other?

Gradually, the characters are fleshed out, the actors' moves are blocked on stage, and the action begins to come together. Meanwhile, costumes are made, sets constructed, lighting designs created, tickets sold, and programs printed. There's an atmosphere of excitement and anticipation throughout the entire company.

Opening night

On the day of a performance, Catherine takes the morning slowly, doing some light physical exercises to loosen her muscles. She warms up her voice and goes over any difficult lines from the play. "I can't eat a lot before a performance," laments Catherine. "I'd be nauseous. I might eat a small meal two hours before the show, something like pasta just to get quick energy. But that's all."

Actors are generally expected to be at the theater half an hour before the performance starts. But on opening night, if it's a big role, Catherine likes to arrive an hour before the curtain rises. She walks around the stage, "just to get the feel of it," before the audience arrives.

Unless the role is truly unusual, it doesn't take long to fix an actor's makeup, hair, and costume. Catherine waits in the dressing room or just off stage, ready for her cue. Like most performers, she gets butterflies in her stomach. "But I look forward to the nervous energy, in a way. That rush of adrenalin just before you go on stage is really useful to actors."

On stage

An actor's fundamental job on stage is to convince the audience that the character is real. There are several different methods that actors use to achieve this result. For example, actors who portray horrible experiences might convince themselves that the event is actually happening to them. Another technique is for actors to think of

One of Catherine's first major roles was in a play called *Saltwater Moon*. There were only two characters: Catherine and Eric McCormack shared the stage for the entire play. "Eric was great to work with," Catherine recalls. "One night, a telescope I was using fell apart on stage. But Eric just added a line about the telescope and the audience never even noticed."

Stage actors usually have to purchase and apply their own makeup. If the role calls for something tricky, such as age lines, the actor might be given a chart to follow. More complicated effects, such as latex masks, are provided for them. But the actors must learn to apply these effects themselves.

Break a leg!
Theater people have a reputation for being superstitious. There is an old belief that wishing someone "good luck" before a performance will actually bring on disaster. That's one reason why actors traditionally tell each other to "break a leg" before going on stage.

something from their own lives that suits the situation. "What's really important," cautions Catherine, "is that if you're going to use ugly memories from your past, then you've got to make sure they're experiences you've already resolved. Otherwise, you might lose control,

and your performance will not be in character."

Unlike film, where a scene can be replayed dozens of time to get it just right, there is no second chance for an actor on stage. A common fear is forgetting or flubbing lines. "I'm lucky I've never frozen," laughs Catherine, her fingers crossed. "I *have* said the lines in the wrong order. And once an actor threw me a line that just

wasn't in the script. But so far, I've never completely blanked."

An actor's greatest reward is the roar of applause at the end of a good performance. "The curtain call is *wonderful*!" exclaims Catherine. "There's nothing like it, if you know you've done well and the audience approves. It's a high that can last for a long, long time."

Catherine discusses her costume with Charlotte Dean, the designer, and with Sylvia Defend, the designer's assistant. "The costume can really help me make the character come alive," notes Catherine.

Vocal warm-ups

Actors often do tip-of-the-tongue exercises to keep their speech precise. How quickly and clearly can you say the following tongue twister?

Steve stored on shelves, six size-seven pairs of shoes, several spotted, spun silk scarves, and sixteen soft, short-sleeved sport shirts.

Activity

Test your acting skills

Actors must lift words off the page and breathe life into them. Two important aspects of delivering lines are intonation and emotional quality. You can test your acting skills by doing the following exercises.

Intonation
You can change the meaning of a sentence quite noticeably by varying the words you stress. This is called changing your "intonation." Say each of the following sentences in at least four different ways by emphasizing different words each time. Explain the

change in meaning that comes from each shift in emphasis.

YOU PUT GARLIC IN THE SOUP.

I THINK THIS PACKAGE IS BIGGER.

MOST OF THOSE PRESENTS HAVE BEEN WRAPPED.

WHAT DO YOU MEAN BY THAT STATEMENT?

HAVE YOU FINISHED ALL YOUR WORK?

Emotional quality
Actors need to imitate a whole range of emotions in their work by changing the quality of their voices. When the emotion is suggested by the words (as in the line, *I'm angry with you*), the task may not seem hard. The following

activity tests your ability to convey emotion without depending on the meaning of the words.

You will need
slips of paper, each with an adjective of emotion written on it (for example: *afraid, amused, angry, bored, confident, hopeful, nervous, relieved, tearful, thrilled*)
telephone book

With some friends, take turns selecting a slip of paper. Don't let your friends read the word written on the paper. Instead, try to show the emotion by reading only the numbers on a page from the telephone book. Don't stop until the others have guessed your emotion.

How to become an actor

Most professional theater training comes after high school or even later. Programs can range from a few days to several years. Courses cover a whole range of subjects, such as voice, movement, and scene study.

The best schools require auditions just to get in. "The first time I had to do a monologue, I didn't know what to do," says Catherine. "I got a book of specially composed speeches, but the artistic director didn't want that. He wanted something from a real play instead."

As Catherine soon found out, it isn't always easy for younger actors to find appropriate monologues. She suggests, "Find a suitable excerpt in a play in which the other characters' lines can easily be cut. You don't have to tell the audition committee you've cut out lines. And if you're good enough, they won't know or care."

Life-long training

Acting school is not absolutely necessary for becoming an actor. "Some people have a knack for acting," observes Catherine. "On the other hand, training never hurts." For one thing, students can make important theater-related contacts while they are in school. School performances also give them an opportunity to show off their skills to agents.

Many accomplished actors constantly take classes to keep their skills sharp. But observing the surrounding world is also vital. "There's nothing that can substitute for life experience," concludes Catherine.

All actors must have black-and-white "glossies" to give to agents and directors. These are page-sized portraits taken by professional photographers.

Is this career for you?

"My father really wanted me to be a lawyer," laughs Catherine. And she was talented enough at debating that law might have been a reasonable choice. But Catherine chose to be an actor, in spite of the drawbacks.

The hard truth is that there are many more would-be actors than there are roles available. Only a few top film stars earn millions of dollars. The average actor scrimps by on a very low income. "An actor can't expect financial security," Catherine emphasizes.

It's not always pleasant

An actor has to be ready to do anything on the job, even if it's unpleasant or stressful. "One Shakespearean character I played had her hands and tongue cut off," reports Catherine. "At the right moment during each performance, I

had to bite on capsules to release fake blood into my mouth. At first, the fluid was so acidic, it actually made my chin raw after only a few performances. So the fluid was adjusted to make it less acidic."

Acting comes first

"Perhaps the toughest part of being in show business," says Catherine, "is that it has to be your first priority." Catherine knows she will have to put relationships and a family of her own on hold, while she establishes herself in the industry. "But for me, anyway," says Catherine firmly, "I just know that if I don't try my hardest at what I want to do before I settle down, I'll never forgive myself."

The job of the stunt artists, shown here replacing two actors, is exciting but may be dangerous if not done with great skill.

Career Planning

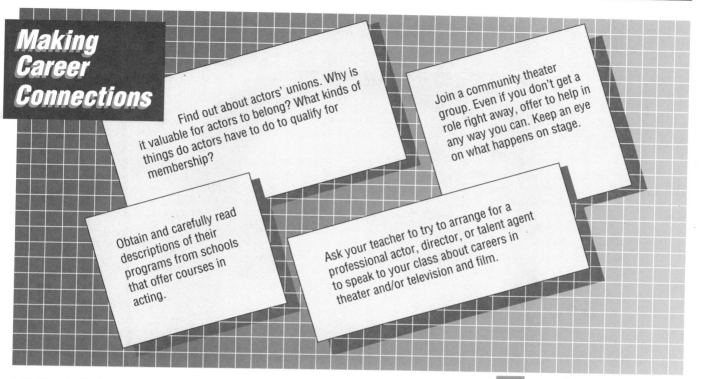

Making Career Connections

Find out about actors' unions. Why is it valuable for actors to belong? What kinds of things do actors have to do to qualify for membership?

Join a community theater group. Even if you don't get a role right away, offer to help in any way you can. Keep an eye on what happens on stage.

Obtain and carefully read descriptions of their programs from schools that offer courses in acting.

Ask your teacher to try to arrange for a professional actor, director, or talent agent to speak to your class about careers in theater and/or television and film.

Getting started

Interested in being an actor? Here's what you can do now.

1. Take theater arts courses offered at your school. Literature, physical fitness, and vocal music courses are also useful.
2. Audition for a school show. Don't give up if you don't get a part on your first try. Keep trying. And if your school doesn't have a drama group, start one.
3. Attend as much live theater and see as many different films as possible. (Consider getting a part-time job as an usher.) Pay attention to how the actors build their characters.
4. Observe people around you. Watch how they react to real-life situations. Pay attention to their gestures, expressions, and body movements. Store these observations in your memory. Or better yet, write your observations in a journal.
5. Read as many plays as you can find. Start a club for reading plays aloud.

Related careers

Here are some related careers you may want to check out.

Announcer
Reads news, service announcements, and bulletins on television and radio. Does "voice-overs" in commercials. May host an entire television or radio show.

Stunt artist
Performs dangerous or difficult routines in place of an actor in movies or television programs.

Acting teacher
Works either privately or in a school, college, or similar institution teaching students acting skills. Coaches performers.

Puppeteer
Performs routines with inanimate figures. Operates puppets by hand, with strings, or in full costume.

Film extra
Works in the background of a film set, portraying various stock characters to add to the realism of a scene. Rarely has lines to speak.

Future watch

There will always be a demand for entertainment on film, television, the stage, and radio. And competition for jobs will be fierce. But there is good news for actors in visible minorities. Directors are increasingly interested in talent, regardless of race, and they are becoming more imaginative in their casting.

Michael Greyeyes

Dancer

PERSONAL PROFILE

Career: Dancer. "My job is to make the most difficult movements and lifts look effortless."

Interests: "I've started to do some acting in films and I find I really enjoy it. When I have some free time, I visit my girlfriend. We met when we were dancing for a company in New York. But we've both moved on, so it's a long-distance relationship for now."

Latest accomplishment: Created two dance pieces, one for a festival in Toronto and one at the request of a Native group in Saskatchewan.

Why I do what I do: "I gained a lot of confidence in myself by learning how to dance. There's something very special about performing on stage. You're doing something that nobody else in the world can do just like you."

I am: Disciplined. "I cope well with tension, and I'm not easily distracted."

What I wanted to be when I was in school: "A criminal lawyer. But by the age of 15, I knew I also wanted a dance career. So I've put the idea of studying law on hold."

What a dancer does

Dance students usually learn several different styles of movement, such as ballet, modern, jazz, and tap. But once a dancer joins a professional company, the work becomes more specialized. Michael Greyeyes, for example, specializes in classical ballet.

"No matter what style of dancing is involved," stresses Michael, "a dancer has to be in excellent shape." For Michael, keeping in shape means taking regular ballet classes. In his company, hour-long classes are held every morning, six days a week. "Either the director or a guest teacher will lead the class," says Michael. "And every dancer in the company is expected to attend."

Each class always begins with a series of exercises called a "barre." "The barre is actually a wooden railing placed at about waist height," explains Michael. "We hold onto the barre for balance as we practice a standard set of bends and stretches." The teacher calls out the different movements and rhythms that the dancers are supposed to follow.

Precision and practice

The barre must be done precisely. Michael carefully controls the angle of his neck, the height of his leg, the point of his toes, the arch of his arm, even the curve of each finger. The teacher walks about the studio making slight corrections to the dancers' bodies, poking muscles or limbs to get just the right effect.

Once Michael has finished his barre exercises, he's fully warmed up and ready to move to the middle of the studio for the next part of the class. The teacher puts together the individual barre exercises to form larger movements. A bend, a stretch, and the lift of a leg that were practiced separately are combined into single smooth movements. Then Michael practices turns, spins, and jumps.

Rehearsal

"Dance class is basically the training of the body," says Michael. "It's a chance to work on muscle reflexes and coordination." The creativity in dance comes in learning roles for performance. The dancer can then add meaning and emotion to the movements. "When you know the music, you can play with the phrasing," explains Michael. "You can hold a movement for a bit longer, or hurry a final step. You use your body as an instrument, just like a musician in the orchestra."

Dancers must memorize all the steps, entrances, and exits for their roles. "When you learn a ballet, it's very fragmented," Michael says. "The work is broken into little sections that are only a few minutes long. And you never rehearse them in order."

Even when Michael is not actually dancing in a rehearsal, he stands quietly at the side, observing every movement. "It's all part of the discipline of dance," says Michael.

In classical ballet, women often wear short-skirted outfits called "tutus" and special footwear called "pointe shoes." Hard blocks inside the pointe shoes allow the dancers to stand on the tips of their toes. Dancing on pointe looks graceful, but it is always painful for the performer.

Dance classes and rehearsals are held in large, bright studios. The walls are lined with mirrors so the dancers can see all their own movements clearly.

All in a day's and night's work

The day before an opening night is one of the busiest for the company. It begins, as always, with a morning ballet class. "You may have time, afterwards, for a drink of water," says Michael, "but then you go right into rehearsals."

For two or three hours, dancers rehearse small sections of the ballet in separate studios. Then the whole company comes together in the largest studio to do a "run-through" of the show. As Michael notes, "It's very important for everyone who's dancing to feel the flow of a show. You've been practicing it in fragments and sometimes you just don't know how sections fit together. You may find, to your surprise, that you're on stage first. Or you may learn that there are only five minutes between two scenes you're dancing in."

During this run-through, the director also organizes where the dancers will stand when they are off-stage. Dancers waiting in the wings need to avoid scenery as it is moved in and out. And they have to make way for other performers who come leaping and running from the stage, sometimes at breakneck speeds.

The company takes a break for dinner at 6:00 p.m. "I'll eat almost anything, as long as it isn't too heavy," reports Michael with a smile. "I'm unusual, though. A lot of dancers don't like to eat at all before a show, except perhaps fruit or yogurt."

Christine O'Leary performs a jump from Michael's latest dance work. Dancing combines strength, grace, and control.

Dress rehearsal

Like an actual performance, a dress rehearsal is usually held at 8:00 p.m. But only the director and a few special guests sit in the audience to watch the action on stage. The dress rehearsal is a performance for the sake of the company members. It helps them learn what needs to be done to make the show run smoothly.

"Before the dress rehearsal, there's a half-hour call, meaning you *must* be at the theater by seven-thirty," says Michael. "But most dancers are in the dressing rooms long before that. There's just so much preparation."

The first job is to apply makeup. Some dancers do this very quickly. Others spend longer, taking the time to relax and clear their minds of worries. As well as applying makeup, ballet dancers with long hair usually have to pin it up. "It can take 15 minutes to get your hair just right," groans Michael. "It can't be the

Some dancers, like Michael, discover they are talented at creating their own dance works. This creative process is called "choreography." Here, Michael makes notes as he listens to the music he has chosen to choreograph.

slightest bit lopsided. You don't want to appear anything less than perfect."

Dressed in loose clothing, Michael does a 15-minute barre plus some jumps and turns in a rehearsal room. He then practices steps for the performance. "You organize this warm-up on your own," comments Michael. "There is no teacher. There may be dancers behind you who will be starting their barre while you're half-way through yours. Somebody else may be just finishing. So it's also a time to focus your concentration."

After warming up, Michael returns to the dressing room and puts on his costume. It's his responsibility to check that all the pieces of his costume are ready well before the show begins. "The last thing you want to do five minutes before the performance is to run around searching for your hat or belt," he points out.

As the dancers are getting prepared, they hear announcements on the PA system. "This is your half-hour call. This is your 15-minute call. This is your ten-minute call. If you're not feeling a rush of adrenalin already, those announcements will do it for you!" says Michael.

The dress rehearsal is run like a real show. If there are any major problems, the director will stop the performance briefly. But it's important to continue. Everyone needs a good idea of how much time they actually have for each scene. Costume changes, for example, may have to be accomplished in a matter of two or three minutes. At the end of the dress rehearsal, the curtain comes down and the company practices the bows. "Usually you're surprised at how the pieces all fit together," laughs Michael. The day has been exhausting, but it feels good to understand the entire show, from start to finish.

The best dance partners react to the music in the same way, passing from one movement to the next in the same split second. Perfect coordination requires long hours of practice.

Activity

Experience music through dance

Just like writing and painting, dancing is an art form. Writers use words and phrases, whereas artists use paints and brushes, and dancers use different movements to represent their thoughts and emotions.

For this activity, you should dress in loose clothing. Find as large a space as possible to move in. A gymnasium would be perfect, but you could also push the furniture aside in a room at home.

Listen to a recording of a favorite piece of music. Choose a short, one- or two-minute section of this music

and play it several times. Let your imagination wander. What images does this section of music bring to mind? What subjects does it make you think of? How does it make you feel?

After you have listened to the music several times, start moving to it. Let your movements represent the pictures you've formed in your mind. As you move, think about the "space," "force," and "speed" of your movements.

1. How are you using the *space* around you? Are you staying in one spot, or are you moving across the room? Are you leaping into the air, or staying near the ground?
2. What kind of *force* do your movements have? Do you think your movements are strong or light? Are they balanced or off-balance?

3. What is the *speed* of your movements? Are they fast or slow? Are you moving with a steady rhythm, or are there sudden changes in speed?

Try repeating this exercise several times until you have found the right combination of movements to express how the music makes you feel. Do you notice details about the music that you were not aware of before you danced to it?

If you wish, perform this dance for a friend. See if your friend can understand the thoughts and feelings you are trying to convey. Or does your friend interpret your movements differently?

How to become a dancer

Michael was only six when his older sister began dance lessons. "I said that anything my sister could do, I could do, too," chuckles Michael. So his parents agreed to enroll him in the class. "I also played hockey and softball. But I enjoyed the dance training most. My teacher made me feel special and encouraged me to continue."

Later, when he was almost ten, Michael auditioned for a national dance school and was accepted. He spent eight years at the school. The training program combined ballet, folk, and modern dancing with a full set of academic courses. For many of those years, Michael was not sure he wanted to dance professionally. But he also did not want to close the door on a possible career.

Once he had decided to be a dancer, Michael trained intensively. For three years after graduating from high school, he was an apprentice with a professional ballet company. It was only then, nearly 14 years after he had taken his first dance class, that Michael got a full-time job.

Computers are being used increasingly in dance. Computer programs featuring stick-figure dancers allow choreographers to experiment easily with different combinations of movement. They can also make permanent records of dance works using these programs.

"If you want to perform classical ballet, you should begin classes as soon as possible," observes Michael. "But older teenagers who develop an interest in dancing shouldn't worry. There are many other forms of professional dance that don't require such early training." Many skilled professional dancers did not begin taking lessons seriously until they were 16 or 17 or even 20 years old.

The kind of flexibility required for dancing is much easier to develop when the dancer is young.

"On the other hand," Michael cautions, "once you *have* decided to pursue a dance career, you have to be prepared to make some changes in your lifestyle. It's not a part-time pursuit. You have to put the time in."

*I*s this career for you?

Dance requires enormous dedication and discipline. "Often you're asked just to follow orders and particular movements," explains Michael. "You must be prepared to perform a step again and again. And not only do you do it, you do it with a smile, if that's what's wanted!"

The major drawback to dancing is the pain from injuries. "Even when you're in good shape, you incur tiny injuries that need some time to heal," Michael reports. "That's why it's so important for dancers to have two days off every week."

Dancing careers are usually very short. Only the most exceptional dancers are still performing in their forties and fifties. And many careers end earlier because of serious injuries. "When you're a professional, there's pressure on you to keep dancing, even when your body is not quite right." Michael should know. He danced on a leg injury for eight months before finally admitting he had to take time off. The leg took a year to heal properly. "This injury could have healed much quicker, if I'd taken a couple of months off at the start," admits Michael.

Dancers tend to be hard on themselves. "If you do something badly, you'll be depressed about it," warns Michael. "But when you do something well, you really savor the joy of it."

Career planning

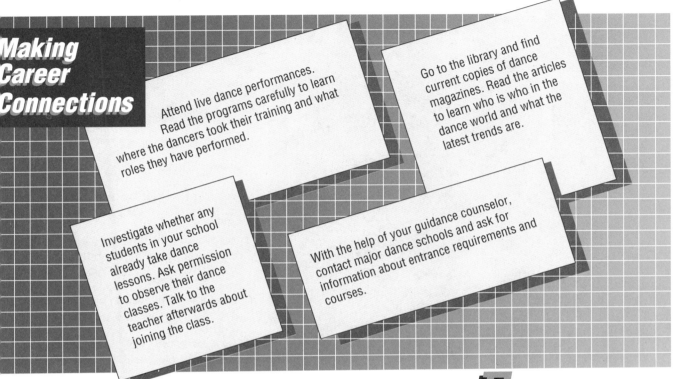

Making Career Connections

Attend live dance performances. Read the programs carefully to learn where the dancers took their training and what roles they have performed.

Go to the library and find current copies of dance magazines. Read the articles to learn who is who in the dance world and what the latest trends are.

Investigate whether any students in your school already take dance lessons. Ask permission to observe their dance classes. Talk to the teacher afterwards about joining the class.

With the help of your guidance counselor, contact major dance schools and ask for information about entrance requirements and courses.

Getting started

Interested in being a dancer? Here's what you can do now.

1. Take dance classes privately or attend a school that offers courses in dance.
2. Join a community dance group.
3. Surround yourself with music. Concentrate on the rhythms, harmonies, and emotions of each piece. Take singing lessons or learn to play an instrument.
4. Keep in shape physically. Classes in aerobics, swimming, and weight-training are especially useful for dancers.
5. Find and watch videotapes of dance performances. View each tape several times, observing the dancers' movements closely.

Related careers

Here are some related careers you may want to check out.

Choreologist
Responsible for noting dance steps on paper, using a special symbol system. Translates the symbols for dancers and teaches them the steps when they learn a ballet.

Dance teacher
Teaches students of all ages how to dance. Usually specializes in one form of dance, such as ballet or modern. Sometimes teaches the folk dances of different countries. May work for an institution or run a dance school.

Kinesiologist
Studies the science of movement. Advises athletes and dancers about more efficient and safer ways to use their muscles.

Dance pianist
Accompanies dance classes. Frequently improvises music to suit movements required by the teacher. Plays for dance performances.

Future watch

There will always be dancers. But they will need to become more and more versatile. Different styles in dance will be blended. Modern dancers will have to understand ballet movements, and classical ballet dancers will need to perform jazz steps. Dancers of the future will have to be able to do it all.

Theater Technician

PERSONAL PROFILE

Career: Theater technician. "In this job, you've got to be able to pick up a hammer, set up a microphone, run a computer. You have to do a little of everything."

Interests: "My husband and I bought a cabin, and we're fixing it up. It's good to be near the woods and the water, to sit on the dock and read."

Latest accomplishment: Designed the lighting for an exciting new dance company.

Why I do what I do: "I never do the same thing twice. Each production is a whole new ball game."

I am: "Flexible, able to think on my feet. And I really enjoy people."

What I wanted to be when I was in school: "I had no idea. I had an interest in the stage. But my first full-time job was as a secretary. Then I took a leave of absence to try a technician's course. Two weeks later, I quit my job. I was hooked."

What a theater technician does

Bonnie Armstrong and her colleagues create the magic behind the shows you see on stage. Theater technicians are part of the crew that is always at work behind the scenes, whether the performance is a concert, a play, a musical, or a dance.

A technician's job is to turn the designs for a show into reality. In very large theaters, technicians specialize in one area: they only build sets, or they only arrange lighting, or they only organize sound. But in smaller theaters, such as the one where Bonnie works, technicians must be ready to perform many different tasks.

Lighting up the stage

Bonnie's favorite job is lighting. "I just seem to have a knack for it," she admits. This job involves arranging and running the lights for a show according to plans made by the lighting designer. "Of course, we have to make sure the audience can see the performers," she remarks. "But it's also important to establish the mood by using different colors and effects."

Even for a small stage, as many as 150 lights might be needed to provide the right look for a show. Each lighting instrument is clamped onto steel pipes located high above the stage and the audience. As Bonnie explains, "The instruments are pretty heavy, and you have to be really careful. All lighting instruments have a safety chain in case the clamp fails."

The lights are hung either singly or in groups called "washes," and they are aimed at different spots on the stage. During a performance, Bonnie controls when each instrument or wash is lit. She also regulates how intensely each light shines.

Sound and sets

If Bonnie isn't operating the lighting, she might be responsible for the sound in a show. This involves setting up audio devices such as microphones, speakers, and playback machines. The sound levels must be carefully mixed and balanced. "There might be as many as four or five microphones for just one set of drums," Bonnie explains. "I have to adjust the volume of sound coming from each separate microphone until the blend is just right."

Technicians also supervise the creation and movement of stage sets and scenery. "This usually requires carpentry skills," observes Bonnie. Technicians have to be resourceful in other ways, too. "Hot glue and tape are the handiest tools in the trade. You're always patching tears in scenery and taping down cables."

When does right mean left?

Theatrical terms can be confusing. The "house" isn't a home — it's where the audience sits. "Stage right" is to the audience's left, and "stage left" is to the right. "Down" means the front of the stage, and "up" means the back. "Props" don't hold up anything. And a "strike" means a lot of work for the crew members who pack away the show.

Bonnie has an overview of the performance as she operates the computerized lighting board in the control booth. Before each show, Bonnie programs the computer for all the planned changes in lighting.

Bonnie's job goes beyond helping to prepare and run a show. She and the other theater technicians are responsible for the security and the care of the entire building and all the equipment in it. They're the ones who are in charge if there's a fire alarm or a power failure. But most important, technicians support the performers and the director in every possible way. "If that means pinning a torn costume at the last moment, or helping to calm a performer's nerves, you do it," comments Bonnie. "It's your job to make sure that the show *does* go on!"

All in a day's and night's work

Bonnie has been on the job long before she dims the house lights and the stage curtain rises on a performance. "If it's a very large show, maybe a band, we'll often start unloading equipment as early as 8:00 a.m.," she explains.

In fact, the schedule for a one-day show can really be quite grueling. Technicians set up equipment and scenery until lunchtime. After a quick meal, they focus the lights. Then Bonnie starts programing the cues on the lighting board. "If we're lucky, we have time to go out for dinner, but often we have to order food in. And then, usually right up until the house opens, we're still programing the lighting cues, plus setting the sound levels and rehearsing any sections of the show that the performers want to go over."

Running a show

During a performance, the most important person behind the scenes is the stage manager. It's the stage manager's job to give the "cues." This means letting the technicians know exactly when they should perform an action, such as moving a piece of scenery or changing the volume of sound.

Bonnie and the other theater technicians are in constant communication with the stage manager through headsets. For example, the stage manager might say, "Stand by light cue 26." "Then," explains Bonnie, "I wait for the word *go*. When I hear the stage manager say *go*, that's when I operate the lighting cue."

Striking a show

After the final performance, the technicians "strike" the set. In other words, they load the trucks, return equipment to storage, and sweep the stage. The theater won't be ready for lock-up until well past midnight.

Sometimes a new show begins the next day. At her own theater, Bonnie notes, "We try to get a ten-hour break between shows whenever possible." But this doesn't always happen. As Bonnie explains, "An industrial show is staged here every January. The first performance is at 8 o'clock in the

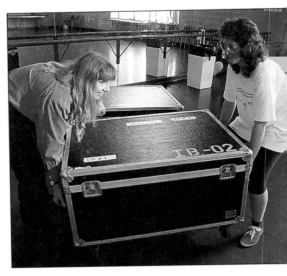

Bonnie helps a co-worker move some road cases. These are used to transport everything from costumes to drums, props to speakers.

Tying the right knot

On smaller stages, scenery is carried on and off into the "wings" — the areas to each side of the stage that are hidden from the audience's view. But most large stages are "fly houses." Scenery is "flown" in and out. This means it moves up and down in the air on ropes or steel cables. Pieces of scenery moved up and down in this way are called "drops." When not in use, drops are stored above the stage where the audience cannot see them. Technicians must make sure all drops are securely fastened, often with rope. The two knots most often used for tying ropes are shown here.

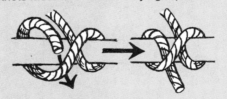

The clove hitch is a fast and easy way to tie a rope to a pipe or a post.

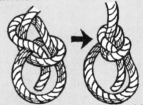

As long as it is made properly, this knot, called a bowline, will not slip, jam, or come untied.

morning. If there's been a show at the theater the night before, there's just no time to go home. So I get four hours sleep in the hotel across the road."

A slower pace

Of course, Bonnie's schedule isn't always frantic. "Sometimes I can do a whole week's work in three days," she laughs. And when a show is in the middle of a run, she doesn't need to come in until three hours before curtain. In that time, she opens the dressing rooms, turns on the stage lights to warm them up, replaces any burnt-out bulbs, and makes any

lighting cue changes the director has requested. "And just before the audience comes in, I shine a few lights on the stage so the house looks inviting. I call it 'setting the magic.'"

Bonnie slips a gel — a colored sheet of transparent plastic — into a groove on a shin light placed at the side of the stage. The term "shin light" comes from the fact that technicians and performers often accidentally knock their shins on these lights. Shin lights illuminate dancers so the audience can see the footwork clearly.

Activity

Creating colors

Color mixing with light is different from color mixing with paints. When paint colors or pigments are mixed, darker colors result. This is called "subtractive color mixing." But when different colors of light are mixed, lighter colors are produced. This is called "additive color mixing." In fact, white light, the lightest color of all, is made by adding seven different colors together — the colors of the rainbow.

If you go on a stage and look up at the lighting instruments, you will notice that they aren't clear white. Instead, they are covered with gels of different colors. See what happens when colored lights are mixed, by trying this experiment with friends.

You will need

three strong flashlights
sheet of white paper
one sheet each of green, red, and blue cellophane
tape

Procedure

1. Tape a different colored sheet of cellophane onto each flashlight.
2. In a dark room, shine all three flashlights together onto a sheet of white paper. Notice that when the three colors are combined in this way, the light appears white.
3. What color is made from mixing blue and red light? Red and green light? Green and blue light?

Challenge

Using only heavy, white paper, a mirror, and a pan of water, design a way to split sunlight into a rainbow. These colors are called the "light spectrum." How many distinct colors do you observe? (**Caution:** Do not look directly at the sun shining on the mirror.)

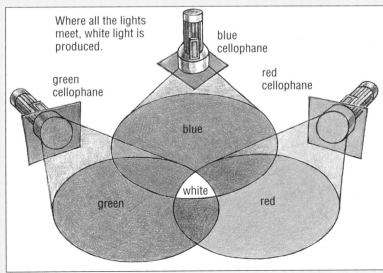

Where all the lights meet, white light is produced.

blue cellophane

red cellophane

green cellophane

blue

green

white

red

How to become a theater technician

onnie was always involved in theater as a student. "I was a volunteer for the local theater," Bonnie recalls. "I began with props and worked my way over to lighting." But it was only later that Bonnie decided to take an intensive course in stagecraft and design.

Many such courses are available after high school. Some take as long as four years to complete. Stagecraft students are often hired for summer apprenticeships. The contacts they make while working in summer programs can be invaluable later, when it's time to search for a job.

Experience counts most

"A course is just a starting point," observes Bonnie. "You can't replace real-life experience." One of the easiest ways to get experience is by working with community amateur groups. "It's not hard to find people who want to be stars," notes Bonnie, "but amateur groups are always looking for help backstage."

Many technicians get their first professional jobs based on the skills they've learned in amateur shows. They begin by "catching call." In other words, they walk into theaters to see if there is any work available. If they're lucky, they'll be hired for a few days or weeks to help set up a show. Then they move on, "knocking on doors" to find new work.

Calls are so frequent and they change so often they're almost never advertised. "You get jobs through word of mouth and on the basis of your reputation," Bonnie explains.

Gobos

It can take a lot of time and skill, not to mention expensive materials, to make scenery look realistic. For special effects, lighting technicians often use "gobos." These are etched metal discs set just in front of lights to cast patterned shadows on the stage. Hundreds of gobos are available commercially in such designs as trees, windows, flames, and clouds. But lighting designers often create their own gobos by cutting tin with an X-acto knife.

Is this career for you?

Theater technicians must be self-motivated. If they aren't lucky enough to land one of the few permanent jobs, they must be prepared to sell their skills. Jobs can last from a few days to a full season. When a contract is up, a technician should be prepared to move on.

Once they *are* hired, technicians must be able to recognize what needs doing. "You have to be able to follow orders," Bonnie cautions. "On the other hand, this is not always a job where you can go in and somebody tells you what you're going to do today."

Theater technicians must know how to work with their hands, doing basic electricity, carpentry, and audio. Technicians can't be afraid of heights because they have to climb ladders and scramble about high above the stage and the house to tend equipment. They must also be prepared to do less glamorous tasks, such as sweeping floors and cleaning paintbrushes.

Working as a team

Most important, good technicians work as part of a team. Members of the entire crew and cast must pull together to stage a performance, often working 18-hour days. This can be hard on personal lives. "During a show, family life often comes second," Bonnie says. "But there are blocks of free time between shows to make up for it."

As part of her job, Bonnie trains student technicians. In this photograph, she shows Terry, a student, how to aim a light called a "follow spot" at the performers, as they move about on stage.

Career planning

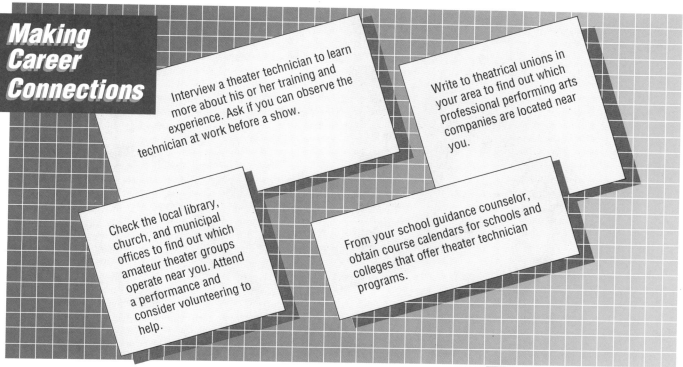

Making Career Connections

Interview a theater technician to learn more about his or her training and experience. Ask if you can observe the technician at work before a show.

Write to theatrical unions in your area to find out which professional performing arts companies are located near you.

Check the local library, church, and municipal offices to find out which amateur theater groups operate near you. Attend a performance and consider volunteering to help.

From your school guidance counselor, obtain course calendars for schools and colleges that offer theater technician programs.

Getting started

Interested in being a theater technician? Here's what you can do now.

1. Take high school courses in applied arts such as carpentry, electricity, art, and shop.
2. Become involved in school productions. If your school doesn't have a drama club, start one with a group of interested students.
3. Join a community amateur group that stages musical or dramatic performances.
4. Attend live performances at professional theaters. Observe the use of lighting, scenery, audio, and props.
5. Contact the technical director of a professional theater to help organize a backstage tour for a group of students. Ask to see how the scenery is moved and how the lights work. Visit the control booth.

Related careers

Here are some related careers you may want to check out.

Property master/mistress

Assembles the props that have been selected by the director and the set designer. Supervises the building of any props that must be custom-made.

Technical director

Hires staff and oversees the entire technical operation of a production, including sets, lighting, costumes, makeup, and special effects.

Prompter

Attends all rehearsals. Keeps a detailed record of all actions on stage. Helps performers memorize and deliver their lines.

Scenic artist

Paints scenery such as forests, city streets, and marble interiors. Must be able to paint in a variety of styles, using different materials. Supervises painting of sets and some props.

Future watch

Computer technology is changing the ways in which stages are run and managed. During a show in the past, a lighting technician might have set a dozen or more lighting switches by hand in preparation for a single cue. Now, the lighting board can be completely pre-programmed by means of a computer. Theater technicians will always be in demand, but they need training to operate sophisticated computer technology.

José Hernandez

Vocal Coach

PERSONAL PROFILE

Career: Vocal coach. "My job is to help singers perform in the style they choose. I can't impose my own preferences on them."

Interests: "I've loved sports all my life. I was a track champion in school. Even today I practice sprinting. To relax, I watch sports events on television. Baseball, basketball, hockey, swimming — I love them all."

Latest accomplishment: "It's impossible to say. I just want all of my students to improve with each lesson."

Why I do what I do: "Music is my passion. I'm a pianist, singer, conductor, and composer, as well as a vocal coach. Coaching helps me understand the whole musical process. There's great pleasure in guiding others to do their best."

I am: "Like a chameleon. When I teach, I adjust to each singer's personality and learning style."

What I wanted to be when I was in school: "It was very hard to make a decision. I was offered scholarships to continue in sports, but I also wanted to be a musician."

What a vocal coach does

As José Hernandez puts it, a vocal coach "tries to create a singer." It doesn't matter what kind of music someone wants to perform. It could be any style — from pop to classical, jazz to country. The most important thing is that all singers have to work on their technique. "Technique," explains José, "is the control that allows singers to perform every day, no matter whether they have a cold, an infection, or allergies."

A vocal coach first assesses a singer's natural range. "In the past," comments José, "people thought that the singing voice was quite different from the speaking voice. But now we know that the basis of the singing voice is speech." A vocal coach listens carefully to determine whether a student speaks in a natural voice, or whether the words are forced too high or too low.

Relaxation is vital

A common myth is that the greatest singers, such as opera stars, need to be large people. "Today, we know that body weight has nothing to do with singing," remarks José. "Singers who are overweight and out of shape often have looser muscles. This helps them to be fully relaxed — which is vital for powerful singing. But singers can also be physically strong and in shape. In fact, they should be. They just have to think a little more about relaxing all their muscles. That's the secret."

Relaxation is one of the most important aspects of technique. It's not surprising, then, that a vocal coach has to be part counselor, as well. "If students have worries and can't concentrate, they won't be able to relax, and I might as well be working alone," explains José. Often a coach must listen with sympathy to a student's problems before a lesson can begin.

José is a blur as he sprints at full speed. A good role model for his students, José runs as often as he can. "Sports are very important for singers," he says. "A performer needs great physical strength to endure long hours of rehearsal."

Teaching and learning go hand in hand

Coaches accompany students with an instrument during lessons. Like many coaches, José uses a piano. Others play the guitar, and José knows of one coach who accompanies students on the harp. The specific instrument doesn't matter, as long as it is a harmony instrument. In other words, it must be able to play chords — two or more notes of different pitch at one time.

Vocal coaches should also be able to sing themselves. As José explains, "When you perform yourself, you are always learning more things that you can teach." This does not mean that coaches sing during lessons. "From time to time I will demonstrate one or two notes," says José,

Ignoring your ears

One of the hardest tasks for a vocal coach is to convince students that they should not depend on their own hearing. "Of course, they need to hear whether they are singing on pitch," remarks José. "But a singer's worst enemy is the ear. To hear their own voices the way the audience does, singers' ears would have to be in front of their faces." Sounds should be focused so that they move out from the singer's mouth towards the audience or microphone. Good singers do not hear themselves very well at all.

"but I don't want to encourage imitation. Students must find their own natural voices."

For José, the most important aspect of coaching is to help singers become their own teachers. As he explains, "Singers cannot call for help in the middle of a performance. So a coach gives them the tools that allow them to determine their own needs."

All in a day's work

Like most vocal coaches, José is involved in many different musical activities. Therefore, he tries to limit his coaching to three days a week. José's teaching days are very long. A typical lesson lasts an hour. "I start seeing students at nine-thirty or ten o'clock in the morning," says José. "I have a half-hour break, and I finish at nine or ten o'clock at night."

Above all, singers need a good supply of air. Thus, José usually starts a lesson with deep breathing exercises, such as those practiced in yoga. José himself learned his breathing techniques from scuba divers who taught him how to survive

As part of his job, José advises his students about which musical pieces would suit their particular voices. His knowledge comes from long hours of studying and listening to different musical scores.

without breathing for three or four minutes underwater. He works with his students until they can easily last up to two minutes without taking a breath. This gives them enormous confidence in their breathing. And

as José points out, "For a singer, confidence is 99 percent of technique."

As well as assigning his students breathing exercises, José also makes them walk, jump, or spin about as they sing. Sometimes he even has them jump up and down on a small trampoline. "People think it's easier to sing when they are standing still. But it's really the other way around," he explains. "Motion liberates the body. Even the ribs move. And once the body is fully in motion, the singing notes are more pure." As with breathing exercises, movement helps to eliminate stress and improve the students' concentration.

Using the diaphragm

The most important muscle used in breathing is the diaphragm. This muscle lies just above the waistline and just under the ribs. It stretches across the body, from back to front. When you breathe in, you lower your diaphragm to allow air to enter the lungs. When you exhale, the diaphragm forces the air out of the lungs.

Good singers don't raise their chests and shoulders as they breathe in. Instead, they purposely lower their diaphragms to allow the maximum amount of air to enter their lungs. The diaphragm bulges down and outwards, much like a spare tire all around the body. Then singers use their diaphragms to force the air out at a controlled rate.

Lowering the diaphragm allows air into the lungs—inhalation.

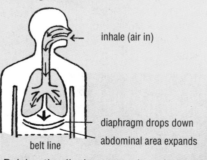

inhale (air in)

diaphragm drops down
abdominal area expands
belt line

Raising the diaphragm pushes air out of the lungs—exhalation.

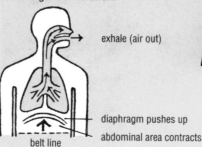

exhale (air out)

diaphragm pushes up
abdominal area contracts
belt line

José helps an aspiring jazz singer to achieve a more focused sound by changing the way she holds her lips and jaw.

Diagnosing problems

Beyond work on breathing and motion, every lesson is different. Students do not always come in for regularly scheduled classes. So it is important for the coach to have a good memory. "You need to make notes, just like a doctor does," comments José. "You must remember the previous lesson and decide what to do based on that."

José rarely plans a lesson ahead of time. What he does in each lesson depends completely on the student's immediate requirements. Sometimes, students bring in specific musical pieces that they will be performing on stage. José plays the piano as they sing, listening carefully for trouble spots. He then diagnoses any

problems, offering advice about everything from accuracy of rhythm to the emotion underlying the words. Sometimes students bring in audio or video tapes of their own concerts. José listens to the tapes and comments on ways in which the performances could have been improved.

Usually, José suggests certain vocal exercises at the end of a lesson. Sometimes he asks students to keep a diary or to paint pictures as a way of understanding color and mood in music. The students always tape-record their lessons with José, so they can go back over the material later and practice what they have learned.

At the end of the teaching day, José will have seen ten or more students. Not all of them are

professional singers. Some are politicians, lawyers, teachers, broadcasters, or other people interested in improving their speaking voices. As a coach, José can never predict what challenges the day will bring.

It's a Fact

Most people can learn to sing well. But there are some things over which they have no control. Singers' skeletons — especially their facial bone structures — affect the quality of their voices. The best bone structures for singers are those that resonate fully, giving a rich, pleasing sound.

Activity

Testing vocal cord vibrations

The vocal cords are two tough, elastic flaps that are about the width of your ring finger. These flaps of tissue grow inwards from the sides of your larynx or voice box (the part inside men's throats that forms the bump called an "Adam's apple.") Humans make sounds by passing air from their lungs up through tubes, past the vocal cords, and out through their mouths. The quality of sound produced is strongly affected by the vibration of the vocal cords.

You can test the effect of the vocal cords by doing the following simple exercise. Place your fingers flat on the front of your throat. Then sound out

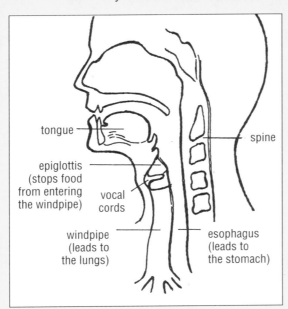

the following pairs of letters. (Don't just say the name of the letter. Actually *make the sound* that the letter represents.)

"f" and "v"
"t" and "d"
"p" and "b"
"k" and "g"

Each of these pairs of sounds is made in almost the same way: the tongue and the lips are held in the same positions. There is just one major difference. For one of the sounds, the vocal cords are close together and the air vibrates strongly. For the other sound, the vocal cords are farther apart and the air passes through without making strong vibrations. Based on what you can feel with your fingers on your throat, for which letter in each pair do the vocal cords vibrate strongly? (Answers are on page 48.)

How to become a vocal coach

Vocal coaches are, first and foremost, musicians. In order to become a vocal coach, you must study music, play an instrument, and learn to detect subtle differences in people's singing.

José began piano lessons when he was four. He worked so hard that he had finished the formal piano curriculum by the time he was 14. That meant, explains José, that "instead of working in a grocery store, I was able to make money playing as a 'repetiteur' for professional singers." In other words, José would accompany the singers on the piano, while they rehearsed for upcoming concerts.

These singers would ask José what he thought about their voices and their interpretations. He seemed to have a gift for understanding the qualities of sound they were trying to achieve. And he had a knack for pinpointing the sources of vocal problems. By the time he was 17, José was so interested in voice that he began to take singing lessons himself. Soon, he explains, "My love of teaching was even greater than my love of piano."

Many vocal coaches do not start music lessons as early as José. They often take formal courses after high school, spending several years studying various pieces and styles of music, as well as musical theory.

Like many vocal coaches, José gains students through word-of-mouth recommendations. People he has taught often tell their friends

about him. Sometimes, singers who hear him at concerts approach him for advice. Some vocal coaches advertise for students when they first begin to teach. But as coaches develop a reputation in the field, advertising is generally no longer necessary.

José sings with his three-year-old son, Michael. José's mother told him he also loved to sing as a child — partly because neighbors would reward him with treats.

Is this career for you?

Do you enjoy music? Do you find yourself listening critically to singers? Do you like working with people to help them improve their skills? If so, this could be the career for you.

A vocal coach needs to know a lot about music and how the voice works. Good coaches listen to a wide range of recordings and performances. They also keep up with the latest scientific discoveries about the human vocal system. And most important, the best vocal coaches have singing careers of their own. This makes them much more sensitive to their students' needs and problems.

Coaching singers requires great concentration and energy. It also demands sensitivity to various personalities and tastes. A vocal coach cannot be a musical snob. The coach needs to recognize the value of all styles of singing.

Finally, coaches should acquire business skills. Some coaches work in schools or musical institutions, but most are self-employed. They must be prepared to deal with the tasks necessary to run any small business.

Career planning

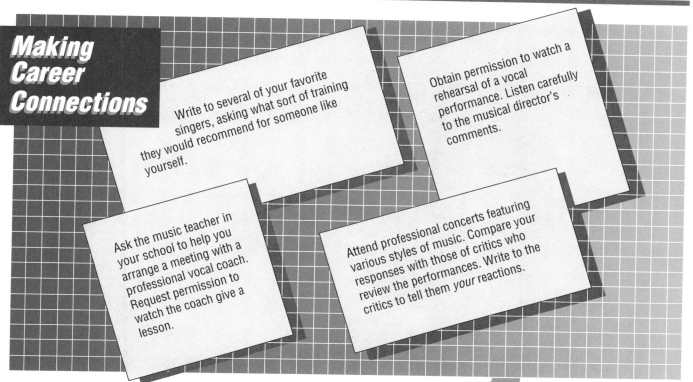

Making Career Connections

Write to several of your favorite singers, asking what sort of training they would recommend for someone like yourself.

Obtain permission to watch a rehearsal of a vocal performance. Listen carefully to the musical director's comments.

Ask the music teacher in your school to help you arrange a meeting with a professional vocal coach. Request permission to watch the coach give a lesson.

Attend professional concerts featuring various styles of music. Compare your responses with those of critics who review the performances. Write to the critics to tell them *your* reactions.

Getting started

Interested in being a vocal coach? Here's what you can do now.

1. Take any classes in music available at your school.
2. Join the school choir. If there isn't one, work with your music teacher to start a vocal group.
3. Try to take private lessons on guitar, piano, or some other harmony instrument.
4. Audition for a community choir in your area.
5. Find and listen to recordings of the same song performed by different artists. Compare the two works carefully to see if you can identify the differences. If you like, keep a written record of your observations.
6. Listen to as many different styles of music as you can: anything from jazz, to rhythm and blues, to musical show tunes, to opera, to hip hop, to oratorio, to pop. Try to describe what makes each style different.

Related careers

Here are some related careers you may want to check out.

Musicologist
Has a wide knowledge of the history and theory of music. Often in charge of programing for radio shows or concerts.

Choir director
Manages a choir or chorus. Auditions and rehearses singers. Selects music and organizes concerts.

Critic
Works for newspapers, television, or radio. Attends performances and writes summaries and criticisms.

Music teacher
Teaches music in a high school, an elementary school, or in a private setting.

Music agent
Represents individual singers, musicians, and groups. Arranges performances, tours, and recording contracts.

Future watch

An emphasis in the future will be on the psychological aspects of singing. Concepts of mental toughness and visualization that are now used in training athletes will become important in coaching professional singers. They will be trained to cope with emotions, to concentrate more effectively during performances, and to make mental pictures ("visualizations") of all their muscle movements as they sing. Singers in all styles of music will turn increasingly to professional coaches for help.

Caroline O'Brien

Costume Designer and Cutter

PERSONAL PROFILE

Career: Costume designer and cutter. "It feels good to look at performers on stage and know that I've enhanced what they're doing."

Interests: "I'm always reading. I love being informed about what others in the world are thinking and doing."

Latest accomplishment: "I've been given a year's leave of absence from my job. I'll be working in Africa for six months teaching women how to sew clothing for the North American market, using their own fabrics. Then I'll study costume design at museums in Paris and London."

Why I do what I do: "It feels like I get paid to play! I've had a thimble of my own since I was seven years old."

I am: Very quiet. "I like dealing with people up to a point. But then I enjoy the solitude of working alone on a costume."

What I wanted to be when I was in school: "For some reason, I thought I would be a teacher."

What a costume designer and cutter does

Caroline O'Brien is in charge of the wardrobe at a professional ballet school. She's in charge of the costumes from start to finish. She designs, cuts, sews, and cares for them.

As Caroline explains, "People working in wardrobe for a large theater do only one job. They create costume designs, or cut patterns, or sew, or dye fabrics, and that's all they do. But in small organizations like ours, one person does several jobs."

Designing a costume

In her role as a designer, Caroline begins work with a choreographer or a director early in the development of a show. "You have to know the mood of the show, such as whether it's comical or serious," she explains, "and also how each costume will be used." If the role is an active one that involves running, jumping, or turning somersaults, the costume must be easy to move in.

A costume's design emerges very gradually. Caroline makes several sketches and discusses them with the choreographer or director. She goes back to her drawing board frequently to make adjustments. "It takes a long time to produce the final sketch."

Like all costume designers, Caroline is very particular about the material to be used. She often calls suppliers in New York or London to find the perfect fabric. Sometimes, she even paints materials to get the right effect. "One costume I designed recently required some very tricky stenciling and hand-painting of the fabric," notes Caroline. "It took a lot of skill because I had to do it after the costume was sewn. One error with the paint could have ruined weeks of work."

Cutting patterns

After a design is finished, it must be "cut." Cutting involves interpreting the designer's sketch and turning it into reality. When she starts to cut a costume, Caroline first takes the performer's exact measurements. Then she makes a paper pattern. "Next," says Caroline, "I make a basic shell that fits the person's body and all of its idiosyncracies." This shell is usually made from a piece of inexpensive cloth, such as fine, soft cotton.

Caroline is at her workbench making a pattern for volunteer sewers. Professional sewers rarely require written instructions such as the ones you see here.

Then Caroline begins work with the final fabric. She drapes the fabric on a "dummy" — an adjustable form that is shaped like the human torso. Using pins and long, loose stitches that can be easily removed, she gradually develops the lines of the costume sketched in the design.

Once the pieces of fabric have been cut, they must be sewn together. Elaborate costume designs often use many layers of fabric and a great deal of hand sewing. "Building costumes," as Caroline calls the process, "takes a long time."

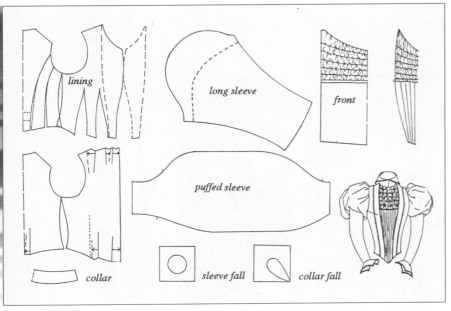

lining

long sleeve

front

puffed sleeve

collar

sleeve fall

collar fall

If a performance is set in the past, Caroline consults books and works of art from that time, to get ideas for period costumes. This pattern is for a blouse made in the 1890s.

All in a day's work

Because she is responsible for many jobs in the wardrobe department, no two days are alike for Caroline. "I never know my exact timetable. I'm always doing things that are different," she smiles happily.

The most hectic days are those leading up to a show. Caroline arrives at her workshop early in the morning and switches on her equipment. One of the machines she relies on constantly is the professional steam iron. "Ordinary household irons that heat up in minutes don't create much steam. But professional irons take half an hour to build up pressure," explains Caroline. This pressure provides the strong jets of steam that guarantee a perfect pressing.

Does it fit?

Caroline may have as many as a dozen performers scheduled for costume fittings in a single day. During these sessions, the costume is

adjusted to fit the performer exactly. But Caroline must also keep future performers in mind. "Costumes are expected to last for 10 to 15 years, and many last even longer," she observes. Therefore, Caroline builds in generous seam allowances and includes many extra closures to permit loosening or tightening of garments. She also cuts hems very deeply so they can be lengthened easily.

When the performers arrive for fittings, Caroline has them stand on a low platform. Mirrors and bright lights help her see exactly how the fabric falls. The performer tells

Everything about a costume — the style of the shirt, the material of the vest, the cut of the jacket, the type of hat — is designed to complement a performer's role.

A fabric sampler

Fabrics are classified in several ways. First, there is the category known as "fiber." Cotton, linen, silk, and wool are all natural fibers. Acetate, acrylic, nylon, polyester, and rayon are artificial fibers. Some fabrics are made using only one type of fiber. Other fabrics, called "blends," are made of two or more types of fiber woven together.

The way in which the fibers are woven together also makes a difference. This is called the "weave" of a fabric. Some of the more exotic weaves include brocade, chiffon, crêpe, damask, moiré, taffeta, and velvet. The "weight" of fabric is another consideration. For

example, wool can range from heavy tweeds suitable for coats, to a very light challis for shirts. And apart from solid colors, there are innumerable "patterns," including florals, stripes, prints, and plaids.

Create your own fabric swatch book by collecting as many samples of fabric as possible from worn out clothing or discarded furnishings. Ask for trimmings at fabric stores and upholstery shops. Classify your samples according to fiber, weave, weight, or pattern.

Scraps from costumes are precious. Caroline stores them in clearly dated and labelled boxes. "We use the scraps for repairs," Caroline explains. "And if we're reviving a production, the costume usually doesn't fit the new performer. Sometimes we have to build a whole new part of a costume."

Caroline whether a garment works well on stage. Perhaps an armhole is too restricted for a certain movement, or a pant leg is a little too long. Caroline then makes changes, marking the adjustments with pins or chalk.

Handle with care

"Every costume must be treated gently," cautions Caroline. Money is in short supply in the performing arts, and the more elaborate costumes can cost thousands of dollars to make. Sometimes Caroline even asks performers to avoid sitting in their costumes when they aren't on stage. Sitting can stretch delicate fabrics out of shape, causing unnecessary wear to a garment.

Caroline fits Bei Di Sheng, a young dancer. Check your favorite outfit. If you grow out of it, is there enough fabric in the seams for it to be adjusted to your new shape?

If a role is being shared by two performers, as often happens in ballet and opera, Caroline needs to fit the garment each day, altering it for the performer who will be on stage that evening. "That's why we ask the

directors to cast people who are approximately the same size," explains Caroline. "We just don't have time to make major adjustments each day. And it's hard on the fabric."

Between fittings, Caroline sews new seams, adds new hooks, and presses out wrinkles. As show time approaches, people stream in and out of the workshop, adding to the general chaos of threads, fabrics, and whirring machines. "I love the adrenalin," laughs Caroline. "There's a real high in performance, and I get completely caught up in the energy."

It's a Fact

People aren't symmetrical: one hip bone may be lower than the other, one forearm longer, or one leg shorter. Almost everybody has one shoulder that is higher than the other. All of these differences affect the line of a costume and how the fabric will fall.

Activity

Re-create a pattern

Making any piece of clothing requires cutting and sewing a flat piece of fabric so it fits the three-dimensional shape of the human body. Usually this is done with a pattern. In this activity, you will reverse the process. You will start with a piece of finished clothing and use it to re-create the original pattern.

Find a discarded blouse or shirt, the more complex in design the better. Check to see how well or how poorly it fits you. Then, using fine scissors or a special tool called a seam ripper, take the garment apart, stitch by stitch. Once you have separated all the pieces of fabric, iron them flat, being careful with the hot iron. Pin the fabric pieces onto large sheets of tissue or newspaper. Outline the shapes in felt pen and then remove the fabric from the paper.

You have now re-created the basic pattern made by the cutter. What alterations could you make to improve how the garment fits? How would you change the design to better suit your taste?

A seam ripper is designed to cut stitches rapidly.

How to become a costume designer and cutter

aroline has always had an interest in sewing. "I started sewing by hand when I was six. By the time I was 11, I was using a machine and making clothes for friends," she recalls. But when she was a teenager, Caroline never thought of sewing as a possible career.

The turning point came while she was studying English after high school. Caroline was invited on a tour of a community theater. She spoke to one of the cutters in the wardrobe to see if they needed an extra hand. They did. And, as Caroline says, "I rolled up my sleeves and started to work."

That experience made up Caroline's mind. After finishing her English studies, she took a second degree in home economics. "There are many very specific theater and fashion design courses you can take, geared to people who want to do design and pattern cutting," she explains. "But I wanted to have a broader foundation."

Making the grade

Even though she did not take a technical course, Caroline had the necessary skills. Looking for work, she took an employment test at a major theater company. For four

hours, Caroline and several other applicants demonstrated their abilities at fine hand sewing, machine work, pattern matching, and finishing. They worked with small samples of many different fabrics and were asked to use a variety of stitches. "It was *very* stressful," Caroline recalls, "because I couldn't really tell what they were looking for."

But Caroline proved her ability to concentrate and work quickly under pressure. Her stitches were the perfect tension. The stripes and prints matched exactly. And her seams were straight and well pressed. She had won her first full-time job.

Is this career for you?

To be a designer or a cutter, you must enjoy working with fabric. You also need to be creative. But in the beginning, you must be prepared to work as a sewer, putting together other people's creations.

One of the most important things for those who work on costumes, stresses Caroline, is that "you have to meet deadlines. You can't tell someone you're not feeling creative today. You've got to get on with the design and the cutting."

You must face last-minute changes calmly. "It never fails," laments Caroline. "You plan your time up to a show. Then someone in the production throws a wrench in your schedule because the costumes didn't turn out exactly as they'd expected. So you just have to redo the work without argument."

Caroline really appreciates the flexible work environment offered by her present employer. After she finished maternity leave, she was able to bring her son, Ceilidh, to work with her. "I rarely bring him in now that he's walking," she says. "There's just too much temptation here for a child."

Working with performers

As well as coping with deadlines, costume designers and cutters have to deal with performers who are under stress. Often it is the people in wardrobe who are on the receiving end of the tension. Most designers have at least one story to tell about a frantic performer who refused at the last moment to wear part of a costume.

Even though friction sometimes develops between performers and designers, everyone knows that it's a team effort to get the show on stage. The people behind the costumes can feel tremendous pride in their role.

Career planning

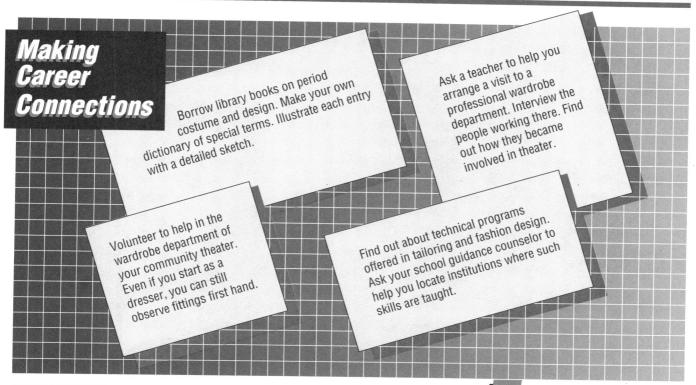

Making Career Connections

Borrow library books on period costume and design. Make your own dictionary of special terms. Illustrate each entry with a detailed sketch.

Ask a teacher to help you arrange a visit to a professional wardrobe department. Interview the people working there. Find out how they became involved in theater.

Volunteer to help in the wardrobe department of your community theater. Even if you start as a dresser, you can still observe fittings first hand.

Find out about technical programs offered in tailoring and fashion design. Ask your school guidance counselor to help you locate institutions where such skills are taught.

Getting started

Interested in being a costume designer and cutter? Here's what you can do now.

1. Practice sewing by hand. Offer to mend any missing buttons, fallen hems, or split seams for your family and friends.
2. Do embroidery. Starter kits are available in craft stores.
3. Make your own clothes using commercial patterns. Start with the simple ones first. Then work your way up to more difficult patterns. You don't have to have a machine to get started. Hand sewing will just take longer.
4. Volunteer to work on costumes for a school show.
5. Take courses that teach sewing skills. Art, English, and history courses will help you learn about period costumes.
6. Take a technical course that will teach you how to use industrial sewing machines.

Related careers

Here are some related careers you may want to check out.

Milliner
Makes hats, headpieces of all types, and, occasionally, masks.

Wig maker
Designs, makes, and cares for hairpieces.

Makeup artist
Creates special effects for performers beyond basic stage makeup. These effects may include fake wounds, wrinkled skin, and deformities.

Footwear specialist
Makes boots, fits shoes, and designs footwear appropriate to the design of a costume.

Dresser
Helps the actors put their costumes on and ensures that all the pieces are kept together.

Future watch

There will always be a need for designers and cutters backstage in the theater. It may take some time to work your way up from sewing. But if you're interested in fabrics, this is an excellent career. Be warned, though. Don't ever expect to make much money. Your rewards will be variety, flexibility, and job satisfaction.

George Meanwell

Musician

PERSONAL PROFILE

Career: Freelance musician: cellist and guitarist. "I get to play a whole range of music from classical to popular."

Interests: "I love languages. I've studied Chinese, and I have a working knowledge of Spanish, French, and Italian. I really love the English language and how it works. For a while, I worked as a reporter."

Latest accomplishment: "I helped start a musical group called *Quartetto Gelato*. 'Gelato' is the Italian word for 'ice cream.' Our first CD has just come out."

Why I do what I do: "Music is what I like to do most. It doesn't matter if I wear old clothes, or live in a hovel, or even starve. I just have to play music."

I am: Someone who enjoys hard work.

What I wanted to be when I was in school: "As a very young child, I wanted to be a train driver. But I mostly spent a lot of time *not* knowing what I wanted to be."

What a musician does

Like George Meanwell, many musicians do freelance work. They are hired to play music by various individuals and organizations, but they are never sure of what work lies ahead. George once found himself playing Mozart on the cello at a sunrise breakfast for a convention of plastic surgeons. At the other end of the clock, he once played his cello at a midnight gala for students.

Short-term jobs

Of course, George has had many more conventional assignments. Like many musicians, he has performed at weddings and in bars. And he often plays cello for advertisements and television programs.

"Many of these short-term jobs come through word-of-mouth," George explains. "The person who is responsible for booking the job has either heard you play somewhere or else knows somebody who has recommended you." It was just this sort of personal contact that once led to a tour of Portugal with a piano trio for five weeks. The original cellist in the trio suddenly became ill. One of the other members knew of George, and he was invited to be the replacement. "It was really exciting," recalls George, "especially when we performed on Portuguese national radio."

Long-term jobs

Long-term jobs usually go to people who audition. And competition can be fierce. When George tried out for the musical *Phantom of the Opera*, the directors chose to hear only eight of all the cellists who applied. Naturally, George was elated when

Though George is a serious musician, he also has a sense of fun and adventure. He recalls, "I once played in a bar, riding my unicycle and playing guitar at the same time."

he landed one of the two positions for cello. Since then, George has played more than 1000 performances of the show over a four-year period. "It's not at all boring," says George, "if you try to play as well as you can. There's always something you can think about in terms of your own technique."

George does not have to play every single performance of the show. He has a standard contract that allows him to hire a substitute privately to take his place when he needs to be away. This was important during the two seasons George also played cello for a dance company. When schedules conflicted, George hired a substitute to cover his work in the musical.

George also enjoys getting together to play music with other musicians who have similar tastes. When he was first starting out, he belonged to a pop trio. More recently, he plays cello and classical guitar with an oboe quartet.

George and the other members of the Quartetto Gelato — Cynthia Steljes, Peter De Sotto, and Claudio Vena — practice together two days a week. "I think of this quartet as being like a band," George smiles. "As well as performing together, we really enjoy each other's company."

it live?

e music you hear on a CD, a record, or a tape is rely one straight performance. Recording ngineers choose the best parts of two or three ersions and stitch them together. They can replace ven a single note that's out of tune. Consequently, udiences expect perfect performances. "But that's what makes live playing so exciting," George insists. "You're trying to achieve perfection. And sometimes you even get close to it."

All in a day's work

On the days when there are two shows of *Phantom* to perform, George starts working at his music no later than 9:30 a.m. "I try to put in as much practice as possible," he explains. That means an hour and a half on his instrument at the very least.

Practice makes perfect

George begins his practice sessions with scales. "These are incredibly important, especially for stringed instruments like violins and cellos," he emphasizes. "You have to know precisely where to place your fingers on the strings in order to get the exact note required by the music." Playing scales also helps keep the fingers limber and improves a musician's rhythm and tone.

George then moves on to rehearse any music he is scheduled to perform in the future. "It's not possible to overprepare," he observes. "But it took me a long time to realize that I should only practice tricky sections of the music. There is no point in playing a piece through entirely, time after time, if only five percent of it gives me trouble."

Working in the pit

After a quick lunch, George drives down to the theater. "I like to be in the orchestra pit at least 20 minutes before the show starts at two o'clock," he says. George tunes his cello, warms up with a few scales, and greets the other musicians as they arrive.

As the house lights dim, there is a sense of energy and anticipation in the orchestra pit. The conductor walks briskly to the podium to the sound of applause. At the conductor's nod, the oboist plays an "A." The orchestra members use this note to check the tuning on their instruments one last time. The conductor raises the baton. All the musicians regard the signal intently. And with a decisive motion of the conductor's hand, the show begins.

Working in an orchestra pit can be exciting, especially when the musicians are working well together. On the other hand, it does have its disadvantages. The noise is so tremendous that it's sometimes impossible to hear your own instrument. The air can be stuffy, especially in shows that use special effects such as dry ice and fire. The carbon dioxide from these special effects is heavier than air, so it tends to slide down into the pit and it can make breathing difficult.

There's also the constant danger of something falling from the stage.

Rock musicians often play electrical instruments, such as the electric guitar or the keyboard. Electric guitars have a wider range of sound than the traditional "acoustic" guitars that George plays.

Hitting the right note

"It takes a lot of practice and careful listening to educate your ear for tuning," remarks George. However, there is always room for disagreement. "In our quartet, we argue about tuning all the time. We use electronic tuners to help settle disputes. But even tuners don't always reflect the finest changes in pitch detected by the human ear."

"Pitch" has to do with how high or low a sound is. Sound is caused by vibrations in the air. A sound that is high in pitch will have more (and faster) vibrations than a sound that is low in pitch. For example, the highest note on a piano makes about 4000 vibrations in a single second. In contrast, the lowest note on a piano makes only about 30 vibrations in the same amount of time.

George has seen a colleague hit by a heavy post. Another was struck on the head by a bale of hay. "That's a real plus to playing cello," he jokes. "You're under the lip of the stage and free from danger. What's more, you're right by the door, so you're the first one out at intermission."

The intermission is 20 minutes long. During this time, the musicians sit backstage, chatting and relaxing. But it doesn't seem long before the stage manager calls everyone to their places for the second act.

Classical guitar is played with the fingernails rather than picks. "Fortunately, I have good fingernails," says George. "But even if they break at first, they do get stronger with use."

The roar of the crowd

The applause at the fall of the curtain can be enormously satisfying. "There's a real high at the end of a good show," reports George.

George tries to grab an hour's sleep before the evening performance at 8:00 p.m. He rushes through his dinner and returns to his post, ready to repeat the afternoon's work. "You have to be physically strong in this job," he notes. "In some ways, it's a lot like being an athlete."

Activity

Investigate instruments

One good way of training your ear is to learn to recognize the sounds made by different instruments. Nowadays, instruments are usually broken into five different categories: idiophones, chordophones, aerophones, membranophones, and electrical instruments.

Select one of these categories of instruments for research. Use encyclopedias and other resources to make a list of all the specific instruments that belong in your category. Make notes about the size, shape, and special features of each instrument. Include line drawings with your comments.

Listen carefully to current recordings that feature these instruments. Then make a tape of short, 10- to 20-second sections taken from these recordings. Each section should feature a different instrument.

When you have collected several samples, play the tape for your friends. How many of these instruments can they identify? Teach them to hear the differences.

Idiophones are instruments like rattles and bells. The sound is produced by vibrations of the body of the instrument itself.

Chordophones are instruments like guitars and pianos. The sound is produced by vibrating a set of strings.

Aerophones are instruments like whistles and trumpets. The sound is produced by vibrating air.

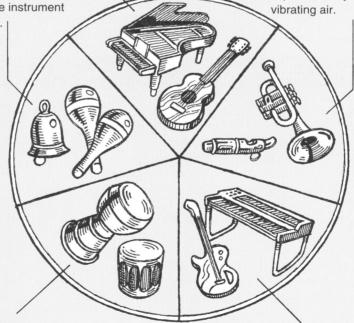

Membranophones are drums. The sound is produced by vibrating a tightly stretched membrane.

Electrical instruments include electric guitars and synthesizers. The sound is produced totally by electronic means.

How to become a musician

George was involved in music from the time he was a young boy. He sang in church choirs. He took cello lessons, both at school and privately. He played cello in the high school orchestra. But George quit taking cello lessons as soon as his parents would allow him. "Playing guitar was what I wanted to do more than anything," he explains. George taught himself to play the guitar by imitating current pop records. And at the end of high school, he briefly played guitar in coffee houses.

Several years later, when he decided that he wanted to earn his living as a musician, George returned to the instrument he knew best: the cello. "I had wasted the time when I would have found it easier to play the cello," he says regretfully. "So now I have to work harder to get the same results as somebody who took the normal route."

The normal route

Becoming a professional musician normally involves studying one particular instrument from an early age. The serious music student should take private lessons as well as those available at school and should practice faithfully every day.

There are many music programs available to those who have graduated from high school. As George points out, "These courses give students not only a valuable education, but also a network of friends and associates who will be very helpful when it's time to look for jobs."

For those who are musical, and who also like to work with their hands, making musical instruments can be a fascinating career option. William Laskin specializes in the craft of making acoustic guitars.

Music students can also improve their skills by taking master classes and entering competitions. Master classes are special lessons offered for a limited time by well-known musicians. Competitions are often sponsored by community service groups or arts organizations. In both cases, students can gain personal, high-quality advice about their playing and careers.

Is this career for you?

Not all musicians are lucky enough to win long-running jobs. As George points out, "*Phantom* really changed my life." He knows the show will close one day. "But I don't panic about that. I've gone through periods of earning no money before. Unless you have a permanent contract with an orchestra or a band, there are *always* times when you're not working."

In fact, a freelance musician's life is not at all predictable. Musicians have to be prepared to travel for work and to go on tours. They also tend to take on as many jobs as are available, just in case there may be none later. It can be very exhausting to juggle several assignments at the same time. To be a freelance musician, you need to thrive on change.

When George spends time with his son, they often play music together.

Career planning

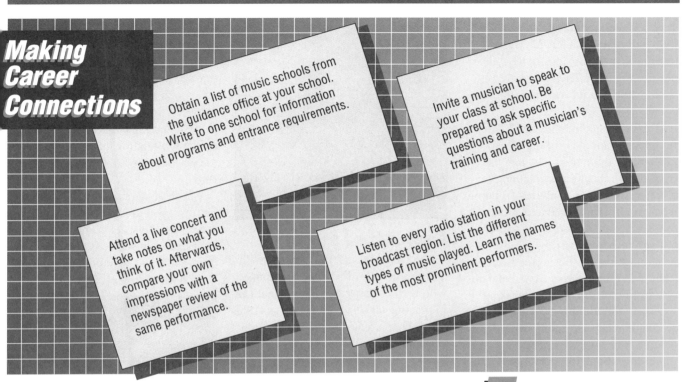

Making Career Connections

Obtain a list of music schools from the guidance office at your school. Write to one school for information about programs and entrance requirements.

Invite a musician to speak to your class at school. Be prepared to ask specific questions about a musician's training and career.

Attend a live concert and take notes on what you think of it. Afterwards, compare your own impressions with a newspaper review of the same performance.

Listen to every radio station in your broadcast region. List the different types of music played. Learn the names of the most prominent performers.

Getting started

Interested in being a musician? Here's what you can do now.

1. Take any music courses available at your school. Join an extra-curricular music group.
2. If possible, take private lessons on your chosen instrument and practice regularly.
3. Get a part-time job as an usher at a concert hall or theater. Talk to musicians you may meet about their careers. Ask them for tips on being successful.
4. Join a community music group. Even if you're not ready to play in a performance, you might be able to act as a page turner or a music librarian.
5. Form a group with one or two other students who like to play music. Work up enough material to give a short concert. You might do this in aid of a charity, or as part of a student council political campaign.

Related careers

Here are some related careers you may want to check out.

Conductor
Heads an orchestra. Often has the final say in the selection of musicians. Chooses the repertoire and sets the tone of the company.

Music store worker
In larger stores, develops a specialization in one particular area of music. Aids customers in making appropriate selections and tracking down obscure titles.

Music editor
Works in music publishing companies, supervising the selection and printing of scores.

Radio broadcaster
Selects, introduces, and comments on music that is broadcast.

Recording engineer
Works behind the scenes with recording studios to produce tapes and CDs for broadcast and sale.

Future watch

Money is usually in short supply for the arts. To entice bigger audiences, concert producers are scheduling programs that include a much wider range of music that will appeal to more people with different musical tastes. Musicians who are versatile and willing to try different styles of music will be more in demand.

Susan Charness — Talent Agent

Do you enjoy putting the right individuals together? Are you intrigued by the business end of the performing arts? Then perhaps you should consider a career as a talent agent.

Talent agents like Susan Charness find performers who fit the roles available for commercials, television, film, or live theater. For example, when a commercial requires a young teenager, brown-haired and energetic, or a script calls for an older person, tall and reserved, casting directors turn to agents like Susan for help. They will telephone or fax a detailed description of roles, plus dates and locations for auditions.

That's when the agent swings into action. "The average agency represents about 100 performers," explains Susan. "They look through their files and choose two or three actors whom they think would be good for the part. Then they contact the performers and advise them about the audition."

Susan's list of performers includes many age ranges, from very young children to older adults.

A specialized agency

Susan Charness is a talent agent with a difference. That's because Susan, who uses crutches herself, specializes in placing actors with disabilities. She started her agency when she realized a television documentary on medical emergencies hadn't used a single disabled performer. Armed only with her nerve and a telephone, Susan called all the casting directors in the city and announced, "I represent Susan Charness Talent Agency for people with disabilities. If you're looking for anyone with a disability, let me know."

Chasing roles

There were almost no calls at the beginning. So Susan decided to make the jobs happen by calling company presidents and urging them to use her clients. "I'm extremely determined and don't know what the word 'no' means," laughs Susan. "Most regular talent agents can't create work. They have to wait for the calls. But because I don't work with the usual clients, I can create work."

As part of her job, Susan also helps her performers prepare resumés, arranges for auditions, supervises the contracts they sign, and develops publicity for them

Susan frequently accompanies her clients to photo sessions.

through press releases. There are always far more performers looking for work than there are jobs. But like every agent, Susan is also constantly on the lookout for that special talent, the performer who will become a real star.

Susan gestures to the mass of photos taped to her walls. "All these people are my clients and have been in at least one show. When they make it, in one small way I make it, too. That's why I love this job."

Adrian Dieleman, one of the performers Susan represents, waits to go on camera.

Getting started

1. Take high school courses in business skills and communications.
2. Apply for part-time work at a large talent agency. If no paid jobs are available, ask if you can do volunteer office work such as filing or photocopying.
3. Get to know the people behind the scenes in show business. Read the entertainment columns in magazines and newspapers. Keep a record of any plays, films, or television programs being produced in your area.

Larry Laforet — Arts Administrator

Behind every successful group of artists are many dedicated arts administrators. These are people like Larry Laforet who deal with the paperwork and public relations that keep an arts organization running smoothly.

Larry studied communications after high school. He worked for a short time in a large business corporation, but when the position became available at a professional school for actors he grabbed the opportunity. "In a small organization like this one," he explains, "I do a bit of everything, which is what I like."

Scheduling

The school offers a three-year training program. Each year, Larry arranges the auditions for the new freshman class. Almost 500 people apply annually for the 30 spaces available in the program. Larry organizes the timetable for all the auditions. Once the 30 students have been chosen, Larry processes and mails the acceptance and rejection letters.

During the school year, one of Larry's main tasks is to arrange the timetable for classes, rehearsals, and performances. "The schedule changes weekly," he notes. "It's a real challenge because we've got classroom and rehearsal space

"We have about 65 students in our program," reports Larry. "And I'm central station for everything, from keeping their schedules straight to helping them find housing."

in several different buildings." Scheduling requires more than good organizational skills. "You also have to be very tactful and try to accommodate everybody," laughs Larry. "Naturally everyone wants to be on the main stage, and that's just not possible."

Publicity

The third-year students at the school spend much of their time preparing for performances. In order to guarantee good audiences, Larry spends many hours on public relations, or "PR" as it is called. "I write press releases

advertising the plays," explains Larry, "and send them to local newspapers and radio stations." In addition, Larry composes and designs publicity flyers, which he then arranges to have printed, folded, and mailed.

Close to show time, orders for tickets begin pouring in. Larry keeps track of the finances, banking any cheques and processing credit card orders. He also allocates the seats and mails out tickets. On performance nights, Larry is hard at work in the box office, selling tickets and distributing the programs he has prepared and printed.

The variety is appealing, but most of all, Larry enjoys the people with whom he works. "Artists are wonderful, exciting, wacky people. Sometimes emotions run high, and you've got to be a real diplomat. But I have enormous respect for what these artists accomplish. And in an indirect way, I'm helping their careers. There's a lot of satisfaction in that," he smiles.

Getting started

1. Hone your business skills. Take courses in keyboarding, word processing, basic accounting, and management.
2. Learn who's who in the arts world. Read the arts and entertainment pages in newspapers and magazines.
3. Take some courses in communications with an emphasis on writing skills.
4. Volunteer to help with ticketing, program production, purchasing, and/or fund raising for a community arts group.

Meg Soper — Stand-Up Comic

If you're always telling jokes and have a knack for seeing the funny side of life, then the career of stand-up comic might be for you. But as Meg Soper observes, "It's one thing to tell a joke in front of people that you know. It's quite another to stand up under lights with a microphone in front of people you don't know."

Meg has always been known for her infectious sense of humor. Not long after she had graduated from high school, a friend encouraged her to perform at one of the weekly amateur nights held at a nearby comedy theater. Her first performance was a disaster. "I was so incredibly nervous, and I found I didn't really have anything to say," she laughs. "But at the end of my five minutes on stage, I did tell one joke that got a good response. It was the most amazing feeling. I knew right then that I had to come back."

Determined to succeed, Meg returned every week for the next two months. During that time, she gradually built up a strong comic routine that was 15 minutes long. "And that's when the manager asked me to become a regular." Meg had moved from being an amateur performer to being a paid, professional stand-up comic. As a regular performer, Meg presents routines several evenings a week.

Word order and timing are vital in telling successful jokes. "You'd be amazed," Meg comments. "A joke can work

one way if you say 'the' at the beginning, and then it won't work at all if you put 'the' somewhere else. And the length and position of your pauses can also make or break a joke." That explains why Meg finds it important to write out and memorize her routines. "Before a performance, I study my lines. Then when I'm on stage, I can focus my energy on the audience."

Preparing new material

Comics find that the most difficult part of the job is writing new material. In the hunt for fresh ideas, Meg reads humorous books. Friends offer her tips for jokes. And, like many stand-up comics, she may hire writers to help her develop material. "I'll present some thoughts on a sheet, and the writers will then decide what ideas they can work into jokes," she explains.

Meg reports that "it's hard to keep adding lines when you have a routine that already works." But she changes her act slightly each week, adding and testing two or three new jokes each time. If a joke gets a laugh three times in a row, then Meg will pay the writer a set fee. A good joke that gets a strong reaction from the audience earns extra dollars for the writer.

"I think a lot of people respect stand-up comedy as an art form," comments Meg. "It's a difficult thing to do, but it's also given me some of the happiest moments in my life."

Getting started

1. Watch the performances of professional stand-up comics. Obtain recordings of their routines and listen to them over and over, until you can recite them from memory. Pay special attention to the timing of the lines.
2. Practice telling stories. Turn your daily experiences into funny stories to entertain your family and friends.
3. Take up debating or any other activity that gives you practice talking in front of people.
4. Audition for the comic roles in plays put on by your school or by amateur drama groups.

Comics use their own life experiences to create material for their routines. Meg's dog, Max, has inspired some good lines that are appreciated by dog-lovers in her audience.

Colin Taylor — Stage Director

When Colin Taylor talks about his job as a stage director, the word "responsibility" comes up often. "As a director," Colin explains, "I have the ultimate responsibility for transferring a play from the page to the stage." This is a responsibility Colin spent several years training for. He was involved in many stage productions during high school, and then, after graduation, he completed a B.A. degree in philosophy and drama.

Colin is now director of his own company. That means he is the one responsible for choosing the plays, hiring the technical and design staff, and arranging casting.

Before they start producing a play, Colin meets with the stage manager to work out the rehearsal schedule and to create lists of props. He also discusses ideas with the costume, set, and lighting designers. But most important, he reads the script for the play many times. As he explains, "If the play is good, it's going to take a number of readings for me to really get the full measure of what the author is trying to say."

Directors are responsible for all aspects of a play. Here Colin discusses costumes with actor Sonia Dhillon.

Rehearsals

Colin needs his script only at the beginning of rehearsals. By the end, he has gone over the lines of the play so many times that he has memorized them without even trying.

Rehearsals usually last about three weeks. "During that time, my primary responsibility is to help the actors deliver their best possible performances," says Colin. For the first few days, Colin leads the actors through the text, analyzing speeches. "This is a very controlled process," he observes. "For example, I might ask each actor to go through the play and find out what each of the other characters say about his or her character." Then Colin gets the actors on their feet to work out where they will move on stage. This "blocking" of the play is very important. As Colin explains, "The way characters move in relation to each other reveals a lot about their intentions and attitudes."

A good director will always try to create a situation in which the actors can work out their own movements as much as possible. "The real challenge in directing is to encourage the individual actors to overcome their fears and unlock their true potential. I try to create situations in which the actors can feel comfortable enough to take risks. Even if their ideas don't work 95 percent of the time, the other 5 percent can be brilliant."

According to Colin, being a director is a 24-hour-a-day job. "Even when I get home after rehearsals, I read the script again. And then I fall asleep and dream about how to make the scene even better tomorrow. So it's a constant, obsessive kind of activity."

For most directors, there's no let-up in this routine. As Colin notes, "When you open one show, you're thinking about the next one." Nevertheless, the job can be enormously rewarding. That doesn't mean there's much money involved. Only a handful of directors ever become famous and wealthy. "I do the job because there's joy in it," says Colin.

Getting started

1. Read as many books and plays as you possibly can, paying special attention to how the characters look, sound, and move.
2. Attend a live performance of a play. Watch carefully how the actors move in relation to each other.
3. Join a theater group in your school or community. Try to get experience in every aspect of a performance.
4. Broaden your knowledge of the world around you. Observe people of different ages and different backgrounds.

Classified Advertising

HELP WANTED

EXPANDING BUSINESS NEEDS PARTNERS
Full and part time. You are: ambitious, open-minded determined to SUCCEED. *No capital requirement.* Send resumé or note to: Box 42, 10020 Albert St. Missinabi, Province/State, Postal/Zip code

CANTONESE/ENGLISH BILINGUAL ACCOUNT EXECUTIVE
LEADING telecommunications company is currently expanding in the Oriental communities. Candidate should have at least 2 years sales and marketing experience in this country. Insurance and real estate experience are an asset. $40,000+. QUALIFIED applicants *only*. Please contact Personnel Dept. Manager, Mr. daCosta at 555-0149

CREATIVE WRITER
Wanted for application at leading telecommunica- nology company. Exp- quired. Reply to VR per. Box 400, The Keenan Blvd. City, Postal/Zip Code

Pharmaceutical

GRAPHIC ARTIS
Our busy Advertising department and lay out flyers, ads and Your related colle diploma is rience that includes liarity wit QuarkXPress. You well und priorities and can wo deadline Please forward you sumé to: ceuticals Trade 489 Su view Ter Zip Code Fax 555-4112 qual opp

ACTING INSTRUCTOR

Opeongo College requires a Acting Instructor for the fall/winter academic year. This is a half-time position for a ten-month contract beginning mid August.

The Instructor will teach both Introductory and Intermediate Acting for 1st and 2nd year students. These courses are University Transfer recognized courses. Possible opportunities to direct College productions exists but is not a job requirement.

Bachelor's degree, acting and directing experience required. Master's degree in a related field preferred.

Deadline for application is June 25. Inquiries can be directed to the Personnel Department
**Opeongo College
450 9th Street
Southdown, Province/State**

CITY DISPATCHER WANTED
Busy City dispatch requires innovative person to run local truck operation. Require good knowledge of ocean cargo. Apply in confidence to: GENERAL MANAGER P.O. Box 4329, New Amsterdam, Province/State, Postal/Zip Code

SALES REPRESENTATIVE

DUTIES:
Promote and sell window and de oducts to the home bu market in the city.
QUALIFICATIONS:
• mum three years sales experience in related field
• An understanding of the cus tom home ma

IRSTLINE HEALTH & RACQUET CLUB

Firstline Health & Racquet Clubs, expanding through Corrale and the surrounding area, offers an exciting and rewarding career in the health & fitness industry. We are currently searching for sales oriented individuals with strong interpersonal skills in the following positions.

1) Membership Consultant
2) Corporate Sales — must have corporate sales experience
3) Program Consultant
4) Cardio Tester

Qualifications:
- Minimum 2 years direct sales experience
- Background in aerobic & anaerobic training
- Knowledge of nutrition

Qualified applicants are invited to call Stan Florry for a confidential interview 555-1305 or fax your resumé to 555-1304

SCARBIN AND REDVILLE GENERAL HOSPITAL
Registered Nurses
In-patient Services
• Full and Part-time
An active acute care facility, the new In-patient Mental Health Department, will provide the experienced mental health care professional or professionals motivated to pursue career in mental health nursing with an ideal opportunity to broaden their group, interviewing, and counseling skills in a supportive and cooperative setting. The background of the ideal candidate will include recent experience in primary nursing care. General qualifications include a Certificate of Competence from the College of Nurses and BCLS. File #42

Recrea herapist
In coop tion with the Occupational Therapist and pri urses, you will de and implement recreati and activiti of all types to individual patient ne essing nt leisure rests. you will ions and pla com ons are availa As the year of experie in an recognized re ion nd Redville Ge ls dedicated to t invited to apply Resources Office S. Scarbin, Prov

Part-Time Usher Needed
Live Lights has an opening for an usher for the coming season. All ushers must be willing to work variable hours, including some Wednesday and Sunday matinees. Successful applicants must be self-confident, yet able to deal diplomatically with the public. Senior high school students preferred. Interested applicants should apply in person, with a resumé, to:
**The House Manager, Live Lights,
123 Forest Street,
Laketown, Province/State,
Postal/Zip Code**

Start Your Own Office Cleaning Business
Be your own boss, part the evening nks For complete information call 555-5190

Weller
JOURNEYMAN MACHINIST
General Machinist, preferably with milling experience required for precision machine shop manufacturing electro-mechanical sensors. Minimum 5-10 years related experience. Must be capable of reading detailed drawings and working to extremely close tolerances.
No telephone calls please. Forward resumés to:
**Mrs. P. Weller
Fred Weller Corporation
34 Leslie Road
Wellington, Province/State
Postal/Zip Code**

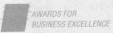
AWARDS FOR BUSINESS EXCELLENCE

Who got the job?

Finding a job

The first step to success in any career is getting a job. But how do you go about finding one?

- In the performing arts, many jobs are advertised by word-of-mouth. Talk with family, friends, neighbors, and teachers and let them know what jobs interest you.

- Respond to "Help Wanted" ads posted on theater call boards and in the offices of arts organizations or libraries, or printed in local newspapers.

- Post an advertisement of your skills on a community bulletin board.

- Contact potential employers by phone or in person. Volunteer your services if no paying jobs are immediately available.

- Send out inquiry letters to companies and follow up with phone calls.

A job application usually consists of a letter and a resumé (a summary of your experience and qualifications for the job). For performing artists, a black-and-white glossy photograph is also required. Applicants whose resumés show they are qualified may be invited to a job interview or an audition.

Activity

Working as an usher

The advertisement shown on the opposite page, for a part-time job as an usher, was placed in the arts and film section of a community newspaper. This job provides an opportunity for anyone interested in the arts to see professional performances on a regular basis. It also offers a behind-the-scenes view of a theater in operation.

The ad directs applicants to go directly to the theater and to bring along a resumé. When applicants submit their resumés directly to the House Manager, they should be prepared to be interviewed briefly on the spot. The first impressions they make will determine whether they have a serious chance at the job.

For the position of part-time usher, there might be many applicants. Two of the applicants were Sarah Eng and Jefferson Buchanan. Their letters and resumés, and the notes made by the House Manager during the interviews, are shown on pages 46 and 47.

Procedure

Make a list of the qualifications that you think are important for a good usher. Now read each applicant's resumé and covering letter, and consider the notes made about each interview. Which candidate has the better qualifications and experience? Whom would you hire? What else, besides qualifications and experience, did you consider in making your decision?

Challenge

How would you perform in a job interview? Role-play an interview in which a friend plays the part of the House Manager and you play the role of an applicant. Then reverse roles. Role-playing will give you practice asking and answering questions. This practice can help make sure that when you apply for a job, you have a good chance of getting it.

Sarah Eng's application and interview

159 Pine Avenue
Laketown, Province/State
Postal/Zip Code

August 27, 19—

The House Manager
Live Lights
123 Forest Street
Laketown, Province/State
Postal/Zip Code

Dear House Manager:

I would like to apply for the position of usher that was advertised in *Our Town News*. I have enclosed my resumé with this letter.

I am especially interested in working as an usher, because I am a serious music student. I hope to have a career as a singer. Working as an usher would give me an opportunity to observe audience reactions and to see a variety of professional performers. I would also like to get a sense of what life in the theater is like.

I have been working part time as a cashier at The Milk Store. I have enjoyed dealing with the public in this job and feel confident that I can use many of the skills I have learned in working as an usher.

Thank you for your consideration. If you would like me to come for an interview, I can be reached at 555-9619.

Sincerely,

Sarah Eng

Sarah Eng

Interview: Sarah Eng
• well groomed
• made eye contact and was enthusiastic
• told about two tense situations as a cashier when customers became angry — handled problems with confidence
• working matinees difficult because of music lessons, but if absolutely necessary will come in

Resumé
Sarah Ashleigh Eng
159 Pine Avenue
Laketown, Province/State
Postal/Zip Code
Phone: 555-9619
Age: 17

Education
Entering final year, West Laketown High School
Employment
Cashier, The Milk Store, 444 Maple Street, Laketown, Province/State
Babysitter: I have cared for the children of several neighborhood families.
Interests
Music
Science

I have been an active member of the Laketown Singers for three years. I am the founder and president of the West Laketown High School Science Club. Our club was the second-place winner for a group science project in the 19— regional fair.

References
Kim Park, Manager
The Milk Store, 444 Maple Street, Laketown
Province/State, Postal/Zip Code
Phone: 555-5235

Alex Weissman, Principal
West Laketown High School, 232 Linden Avenue, Laketown
Province/State, Postal/Zip Code
Phone: 555-3253

Jefferson Buchanan's application and interview

111 Chestnut Park, Apt. 717
Laketown, Province/State
Postal/Zip Code

August 27, 19—

The House Manager
Live Lights
123 Forest Street
Laketown, Province/State
Postal/Zip Code

Dear Sir or Madam:
It was with great interest that I read your ad in this week's *Our Town News*.

I am a theater arts student at East Laketown High School and I plan a professional career in the performing arts.

Although I have never been an usher in a professional theater, I am confident I could do the job well. I have dealt with the public in my summer job at Academy Video Rentals. In addition, I have a near-perfect attendance record at school.

I would be truly grateful if you would give me an opportunity to prove myself.
Sincerely,

Jefferson Buchanan

Jefferson Buchanan
Telephone: 555-4288

Interview: Jefferson Buchanan
- clothes clean, but jeans worn out at knees
- quiet-spoken but confident manner

Why does he want the job?
- knew some of performances scheduled for season, anxious to work for those shows in particular
- friend of former usher, Dale Smith

Resumé
Jefferson Buchanan
111 Chestnut Park, Apt. 717
Laketown, Province/State
Postal/Zip Code
Telephone: 555-4288

Education
19— - 19—   East Laketown High School
- Entering senior year
- Optional courses in theater arts and computers
- Starred as Curly, 19— production of *Oklahoma*
- Member, 19— championship baseball team

Work Experience
Summer, 19— Academy Video Rentals
- Worked as cashier.
- Advised customers on movie selections.
- Conducted inventory and inspection of tapes.

19— - 19—   *Our Town News*
- Delivered weekly newspaper to 47 customers for two years.

References   Available on request.

Index

Answers
page 25: The vocal cords vibrate strongly for the second letter in each pair: "v", "d", "b", and "g."

Credits

(l = left; r = right; t = top; b = bottom; c = center; bl = bottom left; br = bottom right)

All photographs by Catherine Rimmi, except 6(t) Michael R. Guard; 8(t) Fallis, McGuin Management; 8(b) Alison Reid; 10, 11(b), 12, 13, 14(b) Saul Jonas; 14(t) Cylla von Tiedemann; 16-20, 40(t)(r), 41 Kathryn Gaitens; 30(t) RAFY from Zero Patience ©Zero Patience Productions; 32 Gillian Bartlett; 35(b) B.C. Fiedler; 36 Jessica Veitch; 38(t) Brian Pickell; 40(bl) Derek Case; 42(t) Parry Zavitz; 42(b) Shannon Rupp; 43 David Rising.

All art by Warren Clark.